Dreams, magic and life

Jonathon Best

Selected Poems

Selected Poems: Jonathon Best
Dreams, magic and life.
Copyright © 2016 by Jonathon Best
All rights reserved. This book or any portion thereof may not be reproduced or used in any manner whatsoever without the express written permission of the publisher except for the use of brief quotations in a book review.
First Printing, 2017
Paperback ISBN: 978-0-9953520-2-5
www.jbestbooks.com

To my family,
for their endless support, and their endless patience.

Contents

PART 1: THE DREAMER

- CLOOT — 10
- HOUSE OF PROMISE — 12
- MACHINE OF FLESH — 14
- PORTALS TO OBLIVION — 15
- FREAK SHOW — 16
- KEEPER OF THE KINGDOM — 18
- DARK DRAGONFIRES — 20
- FORSAKEN — 21
- OCTOPUS LORD — 23
- PLINTHS OF THE MIND — 25
- DIM DABBLES — 26
- LAST LANTERN — 27
- RUPTURE FARMS — 28
- ELVEN FOREST — 30
- BARD'S TALE — 31
- WHALING STATION — 41

PART 2: THE THINKER

- SHADOW CREATURES   46
- MOME   47
- QUEEN'S CARDS   48
- BEACH OF TIDES   49
- SCHOOL DINNER   50
- 50-50   51
- IF I WERE TO FALL   52
- AVALANCHE   53
- GEM OF THE BEAST   54
- GUITAR MAN   56
- SKY PEOPLE   57
- THE ANGEL   58
- FORBIDDEN FRUIT   59
- MACHINE MARSH   60
- GOD'S GAME   61

PART 3: THE EXPLORER

- WANDERER   64
- TRUE HERO   65
- THE CHOICE   66
- FONTAINE ROGUE   68
- ISLAND LEGEND   69
- A BRIEF HISTORY OF THE APPEARANCE AND DISTRIBUTION OF THE MOST NOTORIOUS BOOK   70
- KING'S TREE   72
- ENDLESS TIME   74
- THE VALLEY   75
- KING'S BIRTHDAY   76
- ELEPHANT'S TEAR   77
- RETIRED WIZARD   78

Poetry from between 2008 and 2016.

This collection is not chronological, but rather separated into loose categories in a way which I feel best tells the journey I have taken over the last nine years.

Part one begins in a dark world of monsters, war and evil. It is a montage of visions, the main source being nightmares, lucid dreams, powerful music, and the lingering atmospheres of some artworks. A few poems retain references that you may recognise.

The second part is my clawing attempt to climb above the gloom. In these poems I explore new ways of thinking whilst questioning the old ones. I feel that this was a rather defining chapter in my life, and it went hand in hand with a large amount of philosophical debates, sociological criticism and alcohol. There's also a scattering of wishful thinking, as I escape to places either off-world or in my own mind, searching for a way to rebuild everything from scratch.

Part the third contains a lot less dreaming. It reflects my love for travel, despite not having a proper understanding of why I do it. These poems are my way of trying to find out why, as well as displaying a few unrealistically ideal outcomes and asking the ultimate question - Is reaching one of those outcomes the purpose of my life?

Part one
The Dreamer

CLOOT

Spreading his wings as he flies to the dawn,
The Inquisitor's binds he shall not mourn,
Can you see, of the land, when you look through his eyes?
When you see, such a land, from beyond his disguise-
Tall mountains rise
As he flies, as he flies-
When the spread of his wings leaves behind his demise.

And over the lands of green,
The ocean's glare in this view none have seen,
And over the nights of grey,
He soars 'neath the stars till the sun brings the day.

Inquisitor came with the marks 'cross his face,
That speaks of blight against the human race,
But could he, just not see, of the world in his view?
If he saw, such a world, would he kill those with few?
His trumpets blew
Through and through, loud and true-
As he poisoned the land that he trampled anew.

And over the lands of spring,
He burnt them alive as they prayed to their king,
And over the towns of awe,
He captured and raped, then he captured some more.

A broken man in the stocks in the rain,
Left to die by disease or the torture of pain.
Can he see, of his life, when he peers at the shrouds?
When he sees such a life he will fly through the clouds-
A figure nearby
Looks on high, asking why,
As he loosed shackled man who then took to the sky.

And over the looms of death,
A rest he shall have once he takes his last breath,
And over the approaching dawn,
The Inquisitor's binds he shall not mourn.

HOUSE OF PROMISE

Where chance had failed,
Children crawl
In search for scraps of food.
Through jumbled concrete
Statured men
Do naught but stir the feud.

A blow to ribs,
Aside you fly,
No longer staining stairs,
That guide the riches
Of the town
Towards their own affairs.

In dark the light
Shone ever bright
Of lonely mansion one.
A frail man
Of gentle heart
Withholds your will to run.

"Come meet the others,
Just inside
And feast through night, we will.
In times like these,
Outside, you'll freeze-
Sit by my fire, still."

A homeless shelter
Fit for kings
As banquets filled the rooms,
But 'fore the dawn
These naive souls would
Find the truth that looms.

The once so crowded
Hall of hopes
Seemed ever thinning through.
Despite the music,
Song and dance
That merrily bled through.

With jolly laughs,
The children played
And ate their faces packed.
While chain and bolt
Slid to their place
Escape no longer fact.

MACHINE OF FLESH

A wretched man
atop grey walls,
Inside a hollowed room.
With holes in roof,
The flooding rain
hid views of tombstone bloom.

The storms approach
Casts fear to hearts-
The citizens of late.
Once lightning strikes
conducting rods
And channels through his gate.

Machine of bone
and rotting skin -
The energies prevail.
Once channelled power
pierced within;
The fungus turning pale.

With roaring cracks,
Once more it strikes;
Alive sparks tortured mind.
He rips from wires -
Crushing straps
To leave confines behind.

And once storm dies,
Against his will,
Apart split thoughts and flesh.
But when returns
the storm's assault -
So will the creature, fresh.

PORTALS TO OBLIVION

From the watch,
He'd travel to Kvatch,
The emperor had sent,
Him to this place
Where more than many lives were spent.

Surrounded gate,
And face to face with fate,
Where smoky ruins burned,
A blooming town
That from fog had their outlook turned.

For in the night,
They came prepared to fight,
Amidst the portals – red,
Oblivion
Did slaughter before they had fled.

So in he'd go,
Through fire and through snow,
To lands of wicked plain,
To stop the lord
Before the worlds fall to his reign.

FREAK SHOW

From the hills beyond the mist
Walked the shrouded man of night,
Through the village 'top the list

Searching for the crippled sight
Of the man he came to free.
In the barred cage, starved of light

There he sat with batons three,
Sobbing in his shredded shirt,
Longing for his chance to see

Life through eyes above the dirt,
But until his master's death
By frozen chains he will be girt.

"Run for home!" whispered the man
While pulling free the shackled freak,
"I've got no food and not a plan

But show some courage, don't be weak."
And quite to the cloaked man's surprise
The hunchback sat and stared so bleak.

"Since long ago I've wished for this
And seen your face form in the snow,
Though now confronted by your hiss,

I cannot flee from all I know.
The master hates me, like the rest
But where am I supposed to go?"

The hooded man unclipped his vest
Despite the cruel winds cutting by
And dropped it in the hunchback's nest.

"Believe me, as I tell no lie,
Oh, one with heart and soul so pure,
If you stay here, then you shall die.

I shouldn't need to say much more."
So to his feet the hunchback stood,
Retrieved the vest from muddy floor.

"Thank you shadow, who understood
The pain of one who is enslaved,
I thought that no man ever could."

Then through the gap, freedom engraved
He stumbled out and passed the tents
And to the hunchback, treetops waved.

His stomach roared at kitchen scents
That carried lightly through the scene,
With final gaze his chest grew tense.

How beautiful his home had been;
he thought now, under star filled sky,
This angle he had never seen –
The angle of those passing by.

KEEPER OF THE KINGDOM

Keeper of the kingdom,
He watches in wait,
For he only knows
How to cross the last gate.
The horses of thunder,
The staves are held high,
Through thick falling rain
Hear the raw battle cry.

The castle a war ground
Barricaded in fort-
Archers of loyalty
Defend with retort.
Boulders are blazing,
Catapults sling,
Young princes protecting
Their father and king.

From graves rise an army,
The un-dead and scourged,
The wizard in question
With the spells he has forged.
The apprentices strike
With the skills they're still learning,
Mimic their masters
For the skills they are yearning.

The clouds, they do part,
As above gods reach out,
With a touch to the earth
The on slaughters shout,
Their powers were draining
And in this they see,
Through the rain and the blood
There was no room for thee.

With a blow of the horn
And a twist of the reins,
Through the gate, they retreat
Over rough muddy plains.
Portcullis is falling,
The drawbridge ablaze,
Though more shall return
And the castle they'll raze.

DARK DRAGONFIRES

With the death of the king
Came the dousing of flames-
Its power removed with the crown.
While the kingdom did sleep
Magick pulsed through their veins,
And carnage set loose on the town.

Through the rain and the wind
The great cracking would sound,
Of space being split into two.
A gate to the black lands
Of demonic pound,
Thrust open as they filtered through.

Fire leapt from their hands
As they murmured quick curse-
Burning as much as they could.
Till the city - a pyre,
Expecting no worse,
And spread to the surrounding wood.

Save the chapel alone
Buildings reduced to ash,
Its shadow cast light on the blaze.
Where the brothers did heal
Those with more than a gash-
Sight dampened by thickening haze.

Then without but a hiss
The events of the night,
Had ended as quick as begun.
With objective complete
And no resisting fight,
They'd left by the rising of sun.

FORSAKEN

Civilians walking,
Their last moments on earth,
Civilians talking,
The day of its birth.
An unknown power
Fabricates inside,
And on its release,
Only he shall decide.

But one is aware,
And within she will seek,
The cure of the night,
From her it shall leak.
Her forces are gathered
Defence is at hand,
Through Hordes of these demons,
Alone she must stand.

The rise of flames,
Lull before scorn,
On this forsaken night
A new realm will be born.
A wave of devotion,
Indestructible power,
Stopping at nothing,
With all to devour.

The barriers broken,
Armageddon is near,
Night skies overwhelming,
The earth filled with fear.
The sorceress fallen,
The demons roam free,
Turning earth that we knew
To the depths of the sea.

OCTOPUS LORD

Monument of
Earth and grime,
Smashed and scarred
From endless time.
Forgotten throne
Left to the shade,
Through hex and curse
It shall not fade.

As darkness falls,
And bells, they ring,
From buried tombs
The spectres sing.
Almighty lord
Awaits first course-
Sacrifice with
No remorse.

Human wails
Reflect through halls,
Ripping tiles-
Cracking walls.
Creeping ivy
Dense and vast,
Holding pillars
Tightens fast.

The lord, now fed,
Turns back to sleep,
But heartless slaughter
Is not cheap.
His arms alight
In acid flames,
As one came forth
From red remains.

With blade in hand
And angered eyes,
The one took flight
Above night skies.
Releasing strikes
Upon the lord-
Forged from thunder,
Dealt by sword.

PLINTHS OF THE MIND

"... Though with each plinth comes an overwhelming mass of power, so closely follows their dark and twisted shadows. Shadows of unbearable consequences, and burdens I can no longer bear. The tree calls for me, as it will call for you in due time. I pray for you, traveller. I mourn your spirit, and can do nothing more than leave you with the same advice I should have taken myself, many years ago..."

With one plinth,
A taste,
Of what was to come.
While playing with fire
Your senses grow numb.

The second,
A rare
But curious thought.
This notion of power
To rarely be bought.

A third plinth,
Façade
Erupts from the skin.
Denying all knowing
While grey hairs grow thin.

With four plinths
Stray forces
Controlling your mind,
Explode in hysterics
Detaching their find.

Bring five plinths
Together
And power untold,
Allow you their usage
To re-shape their mould.

A sixth plinth,
Your soul
Left frail and weak,
While carrier body
Is weeping and bleak.

The seventh
Unable
And not to be tried,
Once all is unleashed,
One may not change their side.

An eighth plinth,
Too late
Your heart can't retreat
To run would be death and
Persistence – defeat.

The ninth plinth
Ecstatic
In bursts of pure might,
Your body a fortress
For winning the fight.

The last plinth
Insanity
Claws through your pulse,
Invincible notions
Seem suddenly false.

DIM DABBLES

One summer's eve
By the hollows shade
Sat a thoughtful, wandering soul.
Like a free black cat,
Though instead of rats
He murdered precious dolls.

With brightened stars
and mountains far,
The moon hung low
on the meadow's green.
A fast escaping sight
that this man had once seen.

However light
his black façade,
A trueness grew within.
This hallowed priest's
untainted heart
Longed for the taste of sin.

Horizon seared,
The swirled morass
of thoughts and shadows merge.
His conscience lurks
a depthless cliff
While howling for a purge.

Macabre to norm,
The insects hum
and birds breathe morning sky.
Though pain desists
There's more to come -
How long can he defy?

LAST LANTERN

Over dry hills
The lions flew-
Hot wind bearing them lift.
With sand in face
And clouded view
The rider held his gift.

Descends the beast
From dunes to trees,
A shrouded forest tall.
Within the haze
Beneath the breeze
Preparing for his fall.

Undying dark
Formed in the air
As branch held back the sun.
A pulsing light
Of yellow fair
Shone bright from lanterns one.

Following paths
The rider stood
And murmur did the light.
"Before our curse
This forest could
Escape awaiting night."

RUPTURE FARMS

Where desert plains to eyes are all,
There stands a factory so grand,
And meat processed by Glukkons - tall.

The biggest plant in all the land.
Though covered by their great success
Is evil within Molluck's hand.

And without caring of the mess
They slaughter all who roam Oddworld,
Native Mudokon's in distress.

Above the window Abe was curled,
And heard the glukkon's plan so bleak,
Mudokons to the farm were hurled.

They would be sold within the week!
Their bones to make a tasty snack,
So far away, Abe tried to sneak.

Alarms were freed in footstep's track,
And soon gave chase, the slig patrols
Who'd find poor Abe and bring him back.

Though not before he'd freed the souls
Of many slaves who worked the farm,
But now he hung above the holes,

that each did lead to oven's harm.
Where Molluck stood aside the slig
And laughed at Abe who spoke his charm.

"The profits from you shall be big!
Our most delicious range of meat,
To beat that of the skrag or pig!"

Though from beyond the furnace heat-
Beyond the mountain range afar,
There came a drumming with a beat.

Encircled at the great altar
Mudokons free did chant their might
And 'cross the sky formed lightning scar.

Then from above the force took flight
Towards the plant all knew so well,
And razed it on that fatal night.

Amidst the dust as towers fell
Small groups of birds could just be seen,
Retreating to the nearby well,

Where Bigface waited all too keen.
The flock of birds he did combine
And Abe appeared where they had been.

Tonight in peace Mudokons dine.

ELVEN FOREST

Three hundred years before
And still the forest heals its wounds,
From man-made, blazing fire
Sending elders to their tombs.

Atop the branches, Sentries
Sound the battle raging horns,
As humans storm through branches,
Weaving in-between the thorns.

Once hunters of the forest,
Now protectors of the town,
Put spear-play into practice
And defend the one of crown.

The skills of elven trackers
Turning them to master spies,
To fight within the ruin
That unfolds before their eyes.

Upon the shore, the warships
Land and set free their machines,
Great monsters of destruction
Driven by those human fiends.

A victory seemed imminent
But little did they know,
Retreat they would from elven lands
Before the month of snow.

BARD'S TALE

"One day at the card table
Below the stairs,
I did meet an old man with
Peculiar wares.
He sat down beside me,
I bought him an ale,
Then we talked of his lifetime
And this is his tale."

There once was a young orc
From valleys of sands,
And his aspirations were
To control the lands.

Once trained with a blade
He was set on a quest,
With his skills so refined
It proved barely a test.

Retrieving the axe head
From caverns up high,
Which belonged to a blacksmith
Who waited nearby.
He had little warning
But felt quite prepared,
And the cavern's own creatures
Had him barely scared.

And once the axe safely
Returned to its home,
The great doors of the town then
Allowed him to roam-

Before he'd depart
A recital was said:
For protection from dragon
'Till he held her head.

Set free to the world,
Now her den he must find,
But at first the recruiting
Of talents defined.

Together in training
Their progress was fast,
But without much more practice
They'd surely come last.

As more was this dragon
Than first met the eyes,
And so many had fallen
Whilst hunting her prize.

The bounty grew higher
Per guild she destroyed,
So to purge her, their pockets
Would be overjoyed.

Then out of the valleys
And into the trees,
They would start their long journey
Of tailing the breeze.
In towns where the hammer
Was likely to fall,
Did the guild offer service
And gave it their all.

As villagers many
Came forth with their pleads,
The would take on the contracts -
Fulfilling their needs.

Experience growing
As ever before
While their numbers increasing,
Though still they'd need more.

So charters were handed
To all men of age -
And together with friends they
Were signed on the page.

The village's chieftain
Blessed them with his word,
As his aid would be needed
From stories he'd heard.

Then final goodbyes
Sent the men further north,
Headed into the mountains –
The home of the dwarf.

In search for the miners
Whose skills with the gun,
Did exceed their poor manners
And speed they could run.
It took some convincing
And many slain trolls,
But at last, now as allies,
They seized their new roles.

"A note for yer leader!"
The dwarven king spat,
Who did stand only taller
Because of his hat.
"You've masters of marksman
And best of the blade,
Though without mighty mystics
You will surely fade."

The mystics he mentioned
Were myth and no more,
Though the adamant dwarves swore
They lived by the shore.

So led by the creatures
That hunters well knew,
They would venture to ocean
To prove mystics true.

The guild left the mountains
And travelled far east,
After long months of searching
They yearned for a feast.

As patience was thinning
There came a great light,
Which did pulse to a chant
From an island in sight.

The orcs and the dwarves
Set up camp on the sand,
Where they built a small raft
To take them to the land.

When nestled the moonlight
They set to the seas,
With a path made of waves
And an escorting breeze.

With beaching of driftwood
Not known to expect,
An unwelcoming greeting
And raft being wrecked.

Before one step taken
In mystical air,
Came a tall elven creature
Who'd morphed from a bear.

"You've waded our waters"
His voice rather deep,
"Though quite safe from outsiders
This island we'll keep."
"We bring no destruction,"
The guild mates replied,
"We have come for allegiance
Before we're all fried!"

Of what they were talking
Elf questioned a dwarf,
While he stood with great caution,
Preparing to morph.

"We speak of the dragon!"
The valley orcs roared,
With their fists thrown to air
As they readied a sword.

And with much hesitation
The elf led them through,
To a well shrouded hall
That from hard ground it grew.

The elders did listen
And covenant made,
As their powers in battle
Would be of great aid.

Before their departure
The elves honed their skill,
Shooting fire at targets
Controlled by their will.

The guild was astounded,
Never to have seen,
Such a display of power,
Despite where they'd been.

Now all were recruited
The guild left the shore,
And they talked of their plans
Of how to win this war.

"With my Dwarven axe
I will slice off her head,
And will dice it to pieces
To serve on fresh bread."
"Don't speak of such nonsense!"
The orc threw a strike,
"She will honour my valley
And be 'top a pike."

And being the wisest
The elf leader said,
"But it makes no real difference,
As long as she's dead.

So to settle disputes
We will take her to shore,
As her blood makes great potions -
We've tried it before."
"But what of the bounty?"
A greedy dwarf asked,
For his hunger for riches
Had been poorly masked.
"The bounty will be split
Directly to third,
To think you deserve more
Is completely absurd!"

"You elves must be dreaming!"
They heard the dwarves cry,
"Our exchange rates are horrid
Where mountains apply."

"Consider the distance,"
Contributed orc,
"As we came from the valleys,
A very far walk!"

And onwards they argued
Till dawn, through the night,
So they slept not a wink
And were no state to fight.

Along with the sun
Rose a black sky of cloud,
Which did bring with it thunder
And rain just as loud.

So refuge the orcs took
Within a small cave,
While the elves ran to forests
And dwarves just stood brave.

The rain turned to hail
And hail turned to snow,
With the guild truly scattered,
Onwards they'd not go.

So center of cavern
The orcs ventured to,
As for there it was warmer
And safe from the flu.

But the group of orcs
Weren't the only to roam,
And they found this dark cave
Was a large creature's home.

Because of the storm
That was raging beyond,
The great dragon awoke
And of food it was fond.
Though when the orcs noticed
It was but too late,
Without dwarves or the mystics
They'd served their own fate.

"But where in this story…"
I asked the old man,
"…Did you play your small part
In this devious plan?"

A laugh he let free as
He finished his glass,
"I was outside the cavern
Well hid in the grass!"

"My presence unnoticed,
As wrote in the plans,
As I come not from mountains,
Nor mystical lands,
But west of the valleys
In thick quagmire swell,
And though of such a distance,
The dragons still dwell."

"And quite like the guild
Had their mission prepared,
The slaying of monsters
Was just what I dared."

"So I followed closely
To ensure conquest,
For her head would be such a
Great gift to the west."

"Though I must admit
When it came to the queen,
I was scared of the skills
That from her I had seen."

"So behind the guild
I would follow close by,
In the hopes they would kill her
With no aid from I."

"And as time flew past
I was rather impressed,
That they found hidden mystics
And passed Dwarven test."

"But all hope was lost
Once the races combined,
As the pride in their homeland
Caused them to tread blind."

"I gazed as they argued
And sobbed as fought,
All the while the dragons
Did laugh at their sport."

"So I took a breath
And prepared for the fight,
If I lingered much more
The guild would die this night."

"So I rallied dwarves
In the best way I could,
With an offer of keg's
To the ones who still stood.
And inwards we charged
To the side of the orcs,
Who were shredded and gutted,
Their bones used as forks."

"The elves heard the battle
And came to assist,
With their raw bolts of power
Discharge from the wrist."

"The queen of the dragons,
Set free her burnt breath,
Which did launch bits of orc
Within flame jets of death."

"Despite dropping numbers
We stood solid ground,
And we left only after
Her body was bound."

"Then I took the honor
Of ending her life,
And her head now a relic
That tells of my strife."

"And that, my dear friend,
Is how this story ends,
But if I have another,
The next time depends."
He finished his brew
And bid me a farewell,
If I'll meet him again, only
Time can so tell.

WHALING STATION

And again as once before,
He watched the lowering hook,
The chains would strain against the mass
As slow, the whale did cook.
With skin – alight,
That gruesome sight,
To lose his lunch
He thinks he might,
But not before
He'd washed the floor
Of entrails left and right.

When all that's left was in a sac
Of skin and melted fat,
He flicked the switched and plugged the hoses;
Ready to extract.
It burst again
'fore he could gain
A single measure
Of the rain,
So as before
He scrubbed the floor
To clean the panels plain.

A clunk as handle twisted free
And open swung the door,
He doubled over, face to sea
And painted rocky shore.
The acrid burn
Where bile did churn
And laughter came
From face, once stern,
Whose watching eyes
Showed no surprise –
'bout time he had his turn.

As sun set low, beneath the clouds
He headed to his room,
But on the way he had delay
As from the forming gloom,
One did appear,
Enticing fear,
Until he saw
The man in clear,
'twas older guy
Who'd chuckled by;
He'd come to lend his ear.

The old had told him all he knew
But still, young asked away,
About this place atop the rocks
He'd no more wish to stay.
With face so brave
But voice of slave,
Some of the answers
He now gave,
Though so aloof
He held the truth;
This island was his grave.

Once knowing too much had been said
The fog whipped old, away,
And left the young man on the rocks
Outside the loading bay.
The doors now chained,
Against, he strained,
But had no luck;
No purchase gained.
He'd sleep outside,
Nowhere to hide
From clouds that growled and reigned.

He planned to find the stern old man
When day broke out anew;
He'd yet to ask him questions – more,
Before the ships came through.
But his surprise
Held no disguise
As what he'd seen
He hoped were lies;
A body there
With greying hair,
Which housed his own green eyes.

Part two
The Thinker

SHADOW CREATURES

Through blackened mist
And sodden earth,
The crows above shall sing.
To the tune of bones
And creaking lids-
Open the coffins spring.

A yawn, a stretch,
The vampires breathe
And look towards the moon.
The red of blood
And smell of fear-
Their instincts are in tune.

With spreading wings
Through nights they fly,
In search for easy prey.
To bite their necks
And drain them dry
Before the light of day.

As full moon sinks,
The shadow creatures
Turn towards their home.
To sleep again
And wait for, yet
Another night to roam.

MOME

When searching was out of the question
And guessing no longer of use,
Take a left or a right?
To be led without sight
Where the optional list was obtuse.

Small guidance would be such a godsend,
Within this most tulgey a wood,
But when one would appear
From afar and from near,
He'd confuse you as much as he could.

And all directions have a sign post,
Many even had two or three,
Some lay far, some lay nigh,
Some would point to the sky,
And others stated "DUM" or "DEE."

To not know the place you are heading,
Meant any path would take you there,
As advice from the cat
Narrowed down to just that,
While his crescent grin hung in the air.

The crossroads would not wait forever,
And now was the time to decide,
The Hatter or Hare?
The Tweedling pair?
From madness she'd nowhere to hide.

QUEEN'S CARDS

From maze of black
And splattered red
Came forth the hearty call.
To not return
Without your head
Mounted upon her wall.

With bat in hand
A path you forge
Through never ending waves.
Fend off the creatures
Of the gorge –
The queens attacking slaves.

Past painted bush
Of bloodied rose
To ends of reaching halls.
This game of cards
To re-expose
The cat beside who crawls.

And once again
His wizened words
In riddles freely flow.
A pointed arrow
Formed from birds
Directing where to go.

BEACH OF TIDES

As waves roll forth
The cages gape
For those who cannot flee,
Upon the steps
wrapped in his cape,
The stranded vs. the sea.

And over shores
A howling wind
Encourages the tide,
Drowning the beach
whose presence thinned-
No place left to reside.

With back to rock
and feet to sand
He gazed at islands near,
While from the sea
a roaring band
Surrounded him with fear.

Within the waves
The ancient beasts
Extended vicious claws.
Dropped to his knees
The stranded feast
was taken without pause.

SCHOOL DINNER

The vehicle cloaked
by heavy fumes,
Its driver turns the wheel.
Guided by dampened
light of moon
And heading for the steel.

Horrific crunch
The vehicle sliced
headstrong through sturdy gate.
Relieving hinge
The driver swung -
Manipulating fate.

Engine engulfed,
Intensive flames
burst from the tank of fuel.
Abandon seat
to solid ground -
Take refuge in the school.

From back of truck
opened the cage
And free the raptors fled.
In classrooms wait
the creatures tall -
Come morning they'd be fed.

50-50

The plates shift,
Splits, my land, in two.
One part fills my memory,
One part still feels new.

Distant, cold, inviting,
Ancestry calls forth.
Always there, awaiting-
Rich and frozen north.

Here is warm and quiet-
Snoring waves on beach,
Desert sands and sunshine-
Nothing do they teach.

Like a new formed iceberg,
Carved out for the sea,
Or a shifting dune of sand
Without identity,
My history is stemming
From more than one home tree.
I struggle to decipher,
Which branches are *me*?

IF I WERE TO FALL

If I were to fall,
Through mattress seams
And wooden beams,
Would the breeze help me at all?
A gust of air
Thrust through my chair,
Would I answer its call?

Into the starry sky,
Past frozen rains
And broken plains,
Would the comets just fly by?
A fiery shard
In my back yard,
Right next to where I lie.

Or to the ocean deep,
Where unseen things
Live lives of kings,
Much like when I'm asleep.
A chasm's drop
Where voices stop
And sonar fails to beep.

AVALANCHE

As such the time slopes gradual by,
Like stone it does momentum gain,
With passing seasons, sun and rain,
Full steam ahead to final sigh.

Within this avalanche of life,
You sell your minutes for a fee
To cast away eternity,
For short term gain and long term strife.

And in the tumble from the high,
Forgotten foes and friends abound,
Would bother not, nor come around,
To bid safe travels or goodbye.

At once, in comfort, quite alone,
Yet plagued by some unwelcome sort,
And girt by what your time has bought-
As dead as all the things you own.

GEM OF THE BEAST

On multiple floors,
The lair does exist,
With beast sat atop –
Her will she does twist.
And strikes at the heart,
Of ignorant those,
Who'd let down their guard
As orders she throws.

So thankfully there
Are passages through,
That link up the lair
In more ways than few.
To carry the slight
Of body and frame,
Who slip past, unheard,
While others take blame.

But one is not all
Of creatures abound,
And any man's eyes
Would see more around.
In tunnels they dwell,
Exerting power,
And any who fight –
They will devour.

Yet hope is not lost
In this hero's tale,
For he would not stray
And he would not fail.
As deep in the lair
Was treasure he sought,
Its value too great
To be sold or bought.

So day after day,
Beneath glaring eyes,
The man slaved away
While cloaked in disguise.
In wait for the gem
To strengthen his heart,
And then, with her hand,
He'd strive to depart.

GUITAR MAN

As I walked the concrete path
Of Human presence aftermath –
A sound pulled me from reverie
And teased my ears a peak.
Midst chattered voices, crowded through,
A lonesome bird, a dog or two,
There came a strum of instrument
that slowed my walk to sneak.

While holding breath I stepped anew,
Upon this ground where nothing grew –
Yet no one else had faltered,
Maybe only I had heard?
I closed my eyes and followed sound
Now resonating all around,
Which led me to a man who strummed
Without a singing word.

Belongings gathered in a pile –
It looked like he'd been there a while,
And planned to stay a while more
Where blankets covered street.
Yet still he plucked acoustic string,
So hopeful on what it might bring,
And all the while a sign requested
Coins, so he could eat.

His chords reflected in me, true,
As from his strumming, sadness flew –
For in his sound I heard the
Weeping sky and Wilting earth.
I asked of that man, quietly,
"How is it that, so clear, you see?"
And in response, his clouded eyes
Said he'd been blind since birth.

SKY PEOPLE

There was a time when trees abound
    Did shape this very world.
Where rivers flowed from all around
    And seedlings, free, uncurled.
There was a time when beasts of old
    Would roam from edge to edge.
Though all before the steel and cold
    Arrived from over ledge.

In pits they landed, stretching free
    And spread like spots on skin.
The uninvited company
    Resembling our kin.
But just how different these men were,
    We'd never comprehend,
Till flattened trees from engine's whir
    Did drive us to our end.

And now they hide behind their walls
    While pumping planet dry.
They siphon off the waterfalls
    To send beyond our sky.

THE ANGEL

His lids grey heavy, melting down his view,
While warming fog pushed merrily its way through.
With empty can now draped in hand
He saw no point to go where planned-
If only he knew.

For in said place so far from comfort's reach,
There was a creature, poised to steal his speech.
With flick of hair and fleeting glance
She'd place him in a moron's trance.
Her gift one could not teach.

Though many tried, none could impress their find,
So soon enough she'd leave them all behind-
The motherland called angel home
'fore finding other lands to roam.
Teasing human kind.

FORBIDDEN FRUIT

And how am I supposed to know,
Of just how sweet this fruit should grow?
The very same that takes the lowest
Branch above my head.
The simple fact is, I should not.
For in this field where they be got,
The only thoughts permitted are
Those written but not read.

Yet as another week rolls by,
There formed an apple in my eye,
The very same that had before
Been waiting in the tree.
Such beauty beamed above the rest,
A seed alive inside my chest,
And now it's taken hold I can't
But watch her grow on me.

MACHINE MARSH

Through the fog,
No movement is seen.
Trees from long ago,
And long ago they'd shed their green.

Shadowed bog,
Vines claim rusted plate.
Piercing sacred ground,
And with them came the forest's fate.

Hear the stream.
Mulling stagnantly.
Ne'er again to flow-
And never will this water flee.

Vivid dream,
Left, from times before.
Fragments 'mongst the damp.
Forever fragments - nothing more.

Wearily,
Children of deceit,
Float up from the depths,
Their murky tears reveal defeat.

Can they see,
With a sight so old,
Through the dead machines,
Where nature, once more, takes its hold?

GOD'S GAME

For part of growing
Is to build
And shape the land of will.
So to the space
The rocks he'll place
And water holes will fill.

Through far and wide,
Great mountains tall,
And caves below are found.
A dash of trees
Bring cooling breeze
And statues built from ground.

Atop, one looks
To supervise
As humans make their tread.
A sheltered home
And fields to roam
While animals are fed.

Extensive grin
He throws the snow
Enthralled by icy pools.
With fire's trace
Put in its place
To warm the frozen fools.

Until the leaves
Fall from the branch
And fertilize the earth.
A beam of glee,
"Again!" says he-
So comes the world's rebirth.

Part three
The Explorer

WANDERER

Through the forest,
The trees watch cautiously,
A hooded wanderer,
Treads quietly by.

They whisper,
Unknowing.
Their bark,
Crawling.

Is this him?

A pause,
Only a moment,
Sniffing the air.
He walks.

Shadow stretching,
Joining those of the trees,
Cold breath hanging,
Glistening.

The forest grows thin,
Lone trees stand weeping,
Thin branches conduct the light,
Illuminating.

In the distance,
A small silhouette,
The moon holds its breath.

Is this him?

TRUE HERO

Through flowing wine
The buoyant man
Did tell his tale of life-
About the day
He'd faced the thieves
And matched them with his knife.

A maiden slung
on shoulder, while
he drew a captain's sword-
Then of the time
He'd tamed the beast
That sold for great reward.

He grinned and laughed,
So unaware
that crowd did dwindle few,
Till one said, "Never
have I met, someone
so dull as you!"

THE CHOICE

The patterns on the ceiling, forming
ghosts of those I knew,
From memories of lifetimes lost
that guide the nights on through.

A densely growing jungle, with
the fruits I would consume,
A beach, a drink, a jet-ski
And bikinis out in bloom.

With islands, archipelagos and
Palm-trees in surround,
You'd think the path well-trodden
But there's treasure to be found.

From trees to mountains - hot to cold -
My legs did rightly lead,
And further into foreign grounds
I let my feet proceed.

Till one day, at a vantage point
that overlooked the world,
A longing came - and I'm to blame -
To go home to my world.

But first I wished for one last stop
Amidst the lands of snow -
A place where if I had been sane
I'd never rightly go.

Then, planning for my future, I
did cast aside my pen,
And take a full time course that taught
me how to live again.

How fortunate! I had been saved,
Before it grew too late,
So with a partner and a job
I followed rules of state.

And everything you'd ever want
was laid before my eyes,
That might have seen if they'd not been
Still gazing towards the skies,

For while amidst the jungles
and the mountains doused in frost,
I'd found a buried secret –
That I'm happiest whilst lost.

FONTAINE ROUGE

And in my wake, a stream obscene
Does stain the pavement 'neath my shoes,
Like Neptune drowning travertine-
From whence it flows I have no clues.

So onwards I, deflated, march,
Whilst fountain gushes, red as red.
The ground an island of debauch,
Where bloated roaches surface - dead.

In hopes escape might mend or cure,
I've tried to flee to lands off shore,
Yet senses don't but amplify.

So, at a loss, before my grave
would fill with blood for me to bathe,
I long for something else to try.

Till answer's found,
I'll drift – unsound.

ISLAND LEGEND

The sun was alight
'bove the shimmering fields
Of rays hitting virtuous sea.
With eyes of delight,
I boarded my freedom
And rescued who waited for me.

Together we'd row
Past the layers of ships
And further past boundaries of earth.
An Island we'd go
Where the beauty did fill
Any heart that could sail her surf.

With blessing of none
As we fled from the world,
Our judgement was our only guide.
To live on the run
From all envious souls-
The ocean was where we could hide.

Was it a mirage?
From the mist did emerge,
A glistening, tropical beach.
Their months on the barge
Was a legend to tell.
Their legend, to no one they'd preach.

A BRIEF HISTORY OF THE APPEARANCE AND DISTRIBUTION OF THE MOST NOTORIOUS BOOK

Among the books embroidered gold,
Where pages tell of stories – old,
There sat a plain and quiet bind just waiting to be
    found.
Despite its presence being new,
The pompous owner thought it true
when quick he answered questions of the book that
    leather bound.

"This holy place, I say, is not
Where books of such a thing be got!"
And promptly he did will away the askers at the
    door.
"If such a thing be not got here,
Then you should double check, I fear,
For I can see it through the window, lying on the
    floor."

The owner scoffed and turned away -
He'd fall for no such trick that day,
As never would he aid those evil pages from the
    pyre.
Though much to his arresting shock,
Upon said book his eyes did lock
And quick would race his heart as forehead started
    to perspire.

He latched the door and tried to find
A place to hide unholy bind,
As people at the doorway peered into the shadowed
    store.
And after just a moment's thought
He realized that if book were bought,
He'd make a pretty pence and be unburdened as
    before.

"Come one, come all, the large and small,
I've plenty books from wall to wall,
And one here in particular you'd be lucky to
    find.
They've printed no more than a few -
Come be the first to read it through;
This book is quite a masterpiece that leather bends to
    bind."

He watched the suckers pile in,
He gave a wink and flashed a grin,
And let the bidding grow as people bartered for the
    prize.
It mounted up to quite a sum;
The rich from all around had come
in hopes to grasp the book with more than just their
    wandering eyes.

As evening set upon the store,
He counted coins and counted more;
The day had turned out better than he ever could
    have planned.
Though as he tucked himself to bed,
A falling object passed his head
And on his wooden floor a heavy leather book did
    land.

KING'S TREE

Where moon that shone so bright above,
Would set alight the darkening sky,
Revealed the monster with no love
Within his heart, unbeknownst why,
That always hunted through the night.

So twixt the thinning leaves on ground,
He searched for one now out of sight
Curled up atop moss covered mound,
Who'd fled again in hopes he might
Spend such a sunset free from pain.

Though just the same as night before,
The monster managing to gain
On crippled man who ran no more,
As ground had muddied in the rain
And twisted legs meant he would fall.

When as the man saw monster's face,
He risked a loud and begging call,
For any tree to take his place,
The monster laughed and stood up tall,
And dragged him back towards his cage.

Tomorrow was the final show
Where cripple held the centre stage.
I wish I didn't have to know,
Though he had told me in his rage
How he was treated at the fair.

He thumped the earth and cried aloud,
And what he said I could not bear,
What he must do to please the crowd –
To picture it, my soul would tear,
So, quietly, I wept for him.

Again I heard a shuffled sound,
The cripple merging from the dim
That monster had already found,
And so I acted on a whim –
Through moonlight I began to sing.

The master stopped his given chase,
And looked down at the twisted thing,
Who ran so often to this place
Of trees belonging to the king,
But till today he knew not why.

So as my branches whistled words
And sang with beauty heaven high,
The forest sent it's chirping birds
That joined our song from nest and sky,
And in the dance the cripple fled.

With master too entranced to care,
He dug my roots from flowers' bed
And sent for men with hands to spare
To carry me to empty shed,
Where new attraction drew the crowds.

ENDLESS TIME

Atop the swell they drift,
Splashing, and laughing of memories past.
Endurance knows no exhaustion.

As time drifts forever,
The monsters play below.

Plunging to unfathomable depths,
The waters like air in their lungs.
They race to the cavernous cliff-face.

Great clock of our existence,
Tranquilly frozen in wonder.

Harmonious sensation;
The seabed humming under-fin.
Aquatic creatures glide.

Moonlight never to befall,
Upon this body of time.

THE VALLEY

The Lake,

As wide as the eye can see,

Glinting in the sun light.

The clouds,

Whispering to the hills,

Softly through the breeze.

The bridge,

Its white wooden beams,

Forever reaching over the water.

The mist,

Hangs low beyond the mountains,

Always in the distance.

The creatures,

Play freely by the lakeside,

And soar through brilliant skies.

Valley of heaven.

KING'S BIRTHDAY

Great hall full of people,
The guests and the king,
Performers in practice
The peasant shall bring.

Knights of the table
The king sits beside,
For they are his honour,
His justice and pride.

Music has started and
Coxcomb bells chime,
For the king's birthday,
The jester shall rhyme.

Through large wooden doors
Come tables of food,
Bowls of fresh cow lung
That royal chefs stewed.

And after the feast
Let the jousting commence,
With no shield or helmet
To build the suspense.

As moon begins rising
With the dimming sun,
Festivities close
Though they all had had fun.
His guests venture home
T'was the end of the day,
With a "Long live the king!"
And a "Hip Hip Hooray!"

ELEPHANT'S TEAR

On edge of dry creek's inlet,
A shadow plods on by,
The rider but a silhouette
Against the orange sky.

His colours were in fading,
With tassels ready frayed,
Though none of this could quite be seen
Against the coming shade.

For, blooming in the distance,
Was man and mount's friend, one –
The only other living soul –
They called the setting sun.

And just before its plummet,
Did bring the cooling night,
Atop the sum of all of it-
A tear shed at the sight.

RETIRED WIZARD

Through large arched windows

Mountains stroke clouds in the distance.

A magical presence

Filters through earth and sky.

Trees of the forest grow from spirits passed.

Through large arched windows

Sun casts no shadows on the meadow.

Not far from the hills

The lake houses creatures of all kinds.

Flower's perfume scents the air.

From behind arched windows

The wizard sits, peacefully watching.

A quill in hand

He writes of the world he's created.

Time overlooked atop his tower.

ABOUT AUTHOR

Jonathon Best was born in the coastal City of Portsmouth, England. Inspired by the surrounding castles, forests and caravanning holidays, there's no doubt that his childhood there has contributed a great deal to his fantasy based imagination. Now living in a tin shed in Perth, Western Australia, the contrasting landscapes and lifestyle offer new perspectives and flavours that he can't help but mix into his writing.

As well as writing, Jonathon enjoys exploring new lands, hiking, and having vivid dreams.

To read more poetry, or to stay updated with promotions and upcoming releases, follow Jon on Facebook, twitter or Instagram. All links can be found at jbestbooks.com

Author's note: For purchasers of this paperback version, the e-book can be downloaded for free at Amazon.

If you liked this collection, please consider rating or reviewing it online.

MOPPERS ANONYMOUS

LEON JUST WANTS SOME FAST CASH.

Pizza delivery was meant to be a cruisy job, but a dead customer and a remote controlled assassin soon sours that gravy train. Between outback hideouts and underground bunkers, Leon stumbles upon the shady side of his boss's business.

TURNS OUT, PIZZA'S NOT THE ONLY THING ON THE MENU.

With the Police Company and the Feds pooling resources against him, will this pizza driver deliver himself somewhere far from anarchy's reach, or take up arms with his desperate, pizza lovin' brothers?

A near future, where the city is crowded and the government is watching. Resistance fighters hide in plain sight at self-help groups whilst scraping the dregs of society into their ranks.
The cops, cameras and bar-code branders were bad enough, and that was before the scientists got involved. Luckily, the Pizza Boss has found a way to make a few bucks amongst the chaos.

Moppers Anonymous is now available in paperback and e-book at Amazon, Barnes and Noble and jbestbooks.com

www.ingramcontent.com/pod-product-compliance
Lightning Source LLC
Chambersburg PA
CBHW021136300426
44113CB00006B/445